MARIE CURIE

Richard Tames

FRANKLIN WATTS

LONDON•SYDNEY

Contents

A Brilliant Student   **4**

Pierre Curie   **9**

The Partnership   **10**

The Discovery of Radium   **13**

Nobel Prizes   **17**

Prizewinner and Professor   **18**

Irène Curie   **23**

Scientist to the World   **24**

Find out More …   **30**

Glossary   **31**

Index   **32**

This edition 2003

Franklin Watts
96 Leonard Street
London
EC2A 4XD

Franklin Watts Australia
45-51 Huntley Street
Alexandria, NSW 2015

© Franklin Watts 1989, 2003

Series Editor: Penny Horton
Designer: Ross George
Illustrator: Simon Roulestone

A CIP catalogue record for this book is
available from the British Library.

ISBN 0 7496 5020 6

Printed in Belgium

A Brilliant Student

Marie Curie is remembered as the pioneering scientist who became the first person to be awarded the Nobel Prize twice – as well as 129 other prizes, medals and titles. She also gave a new word to the language of science – radioactivity.

Marie Curie is known to history by the name she took in her adopted country, France. But she was born in Poland in 1867 and christened Manya Sklodowska. Poland in the year of her birth was ruled by neighbouring Russia and no Pole could forget it, least of all anyone who was involved in education, as both Manya's parents were. Her father taught physics in a boys'

school and her mother was the headmistress of a girls' school. The Russians insisted that Polish schools should teach the Russian language and Russian history. The Poles had to teach their children their own language and history in secret.

Manya was a very bright child, who taught herself to read even before she went to school. When the Russian school inspector came round the classrooms Manya was usually the one chosen by the class teacher to answer his questions.

Manya Sklodowska with her sisters and brother. Left to right: **Zosia, Hela, Manya, Joseph and Bronya.**

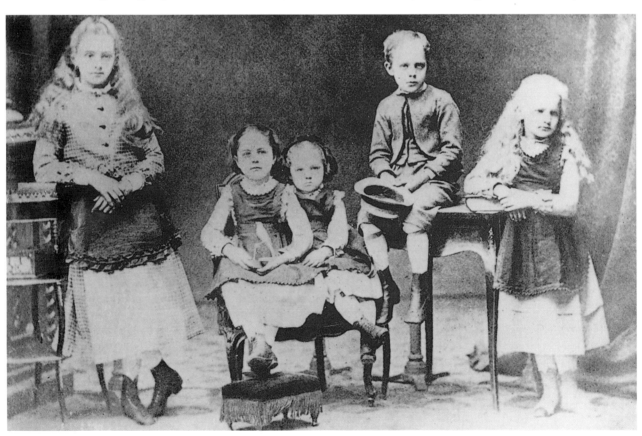

Manya enjoyed learning but her childhood was overshadowed by sadness. When she was six her father lost his job and her family became very poor. Then her mother died of **tuberculosis** and one of her sisters died of typhus. Her oldest sister, Bronya, left school early to take care of the family.

Despite these difficulties Manya continued to work hard at school. When she was 15 she won a gold medal as an outstanding student.

Her father even decided that she was working too hard and sent her away to live on a farm for a year to recover her health.

Although Bronya had broken off her education to act as the family's housekeeper, she desperately wanted to go on studying and become a doctor. This would be impossible in Poland, where women were not allowed to go to university. Many Poles had fled from Russian rule and gone to live in France.

Above: **The Zorawski family house where Manya lived and worked as a governess to earn money for Bronya.**

Left: **Manya, Bronya and Hela with their father, Mr Slodowski.**

So Bronya set her heart on going to Paris to study at the famous Sorbonne University. But, she had no money.

When Manya returned from the country she and Bronya agreed to help each other. Manya would get a job as a **governess** and send her earnings to support Bronya in Paris. Then, when Bronya could afford it, she would help Manya with her education in turn.

Manya went to live in a village called Szczuki, with a family called Zorawski. Besides teaching the two children of the family for seven hours a day, she also organized lessons in her own room for another two hours a day and on her days off. These classes were for poor Polish children from the neighbourhood. Manya spent her evenings and early mornings devouring books on mathematics and science.

When Bronya finally finished her studies she married a Polish doctor, Casimir Dluski. They invited Manya to live with them in Paris while she went to the university. It was a giant step for Manya to leave her family and her country, but her eagerness to study overcame her fear of the unknown. She travelled to Paris in an open railway carriage, even though it was winter, to save on the fare. The journey took three days and all she had to eat were the home-made snacks she had brought with her. But she arrived safely in the great city of her dreams. And Manya quickly became Marie.

Manya (left) **and Bronya** (right) **who helped each other to complete their educations.**

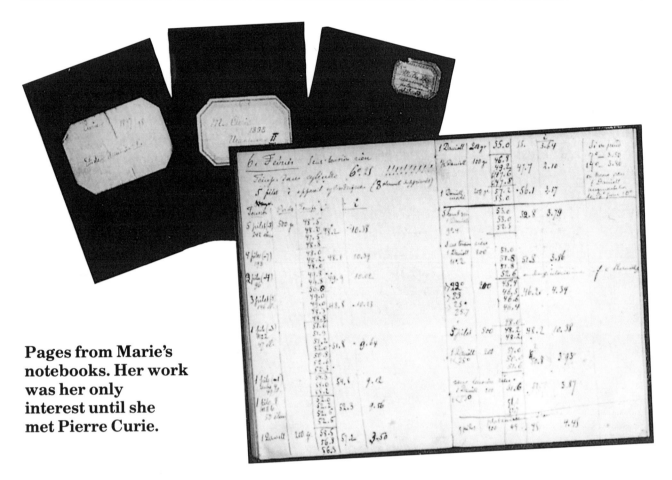

Pages from Marie's notebooks. Her work was her only interest until she met Pierre Curie.

For the first few months, while she improved her French, Marie stayed with Bronya and her husband. But they lived more than an hour away from the university and Marie was, in any case, determined to be independent. So she moved to be nearer her work, even though this meant living in one cold, bare room and eating just enough food to keep her strength up. In the winter things were so bad that she had to study in bed, wearing a coat to keep her warm. But none of this could hold her back from learning.

Marie's outlook on life is shown clearly in a letter she wrote during this time:–

" ... life is not easy for any of us. But what of that? We must have **perseverance** and, above all, confidence in ourselves. We must believe that we are gifted for something, and that this thing, at whatever cost, must be attained."

Thanks to a scholarship, Marie was able to go on studying until she had completed two courses. In her final examinations she came first in mathematics and second in physics.

By 1894, Marie, at the age of 27, had acquired not one, but two degrees from France's top university and become a totally fluent speaker of the French language as well. Soon she would complete her commitment to her adopted country by marrying a Frenchman.

Pierre Curie

Pierre Curie was born in Paris, the son of a doctor. Pierre's father was also keenly interested in research and recognized that his son was an exceptionally brilliant child. He arranged for Pierre to be taught at home, first of all by himself, then by a personal tutor. By the age of 16 Pierre had received the university bachelor's degree in science and by 18 he had a master's degree. At 19 he was appointed a laboratory assistant and began his own career in research. Over the next 15 years he invented a new apparatus for measuring small quantities of electricity and a new ultra-sensitive scale for weighing tiny amounts of material. He also made important discoveries in the science of crystals and magnetism. In addition to this he was head of the laboratory at the School of Physics and Chemistry and taught a class of 30 students. For all these efforts he was paid 300 francs a month, about the same wage as a skilled factory worker.

Shy but gifted, Pierre could look forward to a lonely life unless he could meet a woman to match his own interests and personality. Her name was Marie Sklodowska.

Pierre Curie (standing, right) **with his brother Jacques and his parents** (seated).

The Partnership

Marie and Pierre Curie were married in 1895. It was not a grand wedding. Marie refused to have a special white gown but chose a plain dress instead, so that she could wear it for work afterward. The Curies spent their honeymoon on a bicycle tour of France. It was a very healthy vacation and also very cheap. Cycling was to be one of their favorite pastimes. In everything they did together the shy, brilliant Curies were to be real partners. And their foremost interest, of course, was scientific research. Pierre had made important discoveries about magnetism. Marie decided to follow this up by looking at the magnetic

Below: **Bicycling became the Curies' Curies' favorite way of relaxing.**

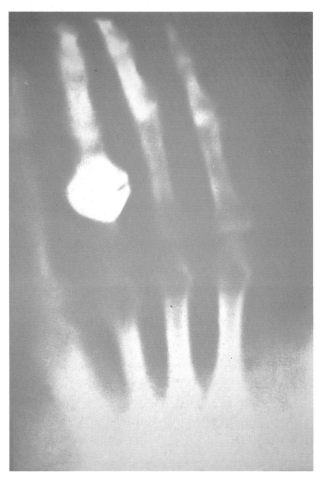

Above: **An X-ray made by Roentgen of his wife's hand in 1895.**

properties of steel.

In 1895, the year of the Curies' marriage, a German scientist called Wilhelm Roentgen made an accidental discovery that puzzled him. He found that certain substances produced rays of energy which would pass through soft materials but not hard ones, like metal or bone. Because scientists often use the symbol "X" to stand for something unknown, he called his mysterious discovery the "X-ray."

But the X-ray was more than an amusing puzzle. By directing X-rays and photographic film at a solid object which consisted of both soft and hard substances, like a human body, it proved to be possible to make a positive image of the hard ones, even if they were completely covered by the soft ones. In other words it was now possible to look inside the human body without carrying out surgery. Within a few days of being discovered X-rays were used to locate a bullet in a man's leg. Medicine had acquired a major new tool for examining the sick and injured.

The year after Roentgen's discovery, a French researcher, Antoine Henri Becquerel, who was a friend of the Curies, found that a rare substance called **uranium** gave off rays that seemed to be very much like the X-rays Wilhelm Roentgen had described.

In 1897, the year of Roentgen's discovery, Marie Curie gave birth to a daughter, Irène. The Curies were very happy about starting a family, but Marie was still determined to go on with her scientific work. So she found someone to look after baby Irène and decided to follow up Becquerel's discovery and make a special study of uranium and the rays it gave out.

Henri Becquerel who discovered that uranium gave off rays like X-rays.

Marie and Pierre with their first daughter, Irène, born in 1897.

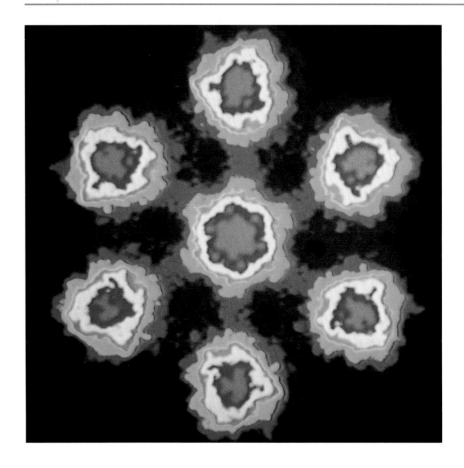

Uranium, seen through a microscope and then coloured to show its structure.

Everything – rocks, plants, animals – is made up of basic substances which scientists call elements. They are the raw materials of our universe. Scientists are able to break things down into their various elements. They can also make tests on each element to discover its various properties. In a small, damp laboratory in the Sorbonne's School of Physics and Chemistry, Marie began a long and painstaking series of experiments, testing every element then known to science. She found out that only two elements – uranium and **thorium** – gave off rays like the ones Becquerel had described. Marie invented a new name for this property of giving off rays of energy – radioactivity.

Marie then made another important discovery about a **mineral** called pitchblende, a black substance, rather like stiff tar, which contains tiny quantities of uranium but no thorium. She found that pitchblende gave off eight times more rays than the uranium it contained. It was, to use her own new term, more radioactive. Marie reasoned that pitchblende must therefore contain another element, which was also radioactive but which no one had, as yet, discovered. Pierre was so excited by Marie's discovery that he decided to give up his own work and join her in her research to find out more about this new element. They decided to call it radium.

The Discovery of Radium

Marie already realized that the new element, simply because it had not been detected so far, was only likely to be found in pitchblende in minute quantities. To isolate any amount large enough to test and measure, Marie would need huge amounts of pitchblende – and even more perseverance. People usually imagine scientific research means making minute observations with delicate instruments; and this is often the case. But Marie's efforts to isolate radium from pitchblende were more like heavy labouring as she heated and stirred great pots of the sticky stuff, **purifying** it and taking out more and more of its various elements for Pierre to identify and analyse. In the course of her work Marie discovered another unknown element which was not radioactive and not therefore radium. She decided to call it polonium in honour of her native country. Polonia is the Polish name for Poland.

Even while she was working on her experiments Marie took on another job – teaching physics at the Ecole Normale Supérieure in Sèvres in the southwest of Paris.

To isolate radium, Marie stirred huge pots of pitchblende, while Pierre analysed its elements.

Marie's own experiments were now being carried out in an abandoned wooden shed, furnished with old kitchen tables, a cast-iron stove and a blackboard. But she was later to write that:–

" ... it was in this miserable old shed that the best and happiest years of our life were spent, entirely **consecrated** to work. I sometimes passed the whole day stirring a boiling mass with an iron rod nearly as big as myself. In the evening I was entirely broken with fatigue."

Above right: **The old wooden shed, at the School of Physics, where radium was discovered.**

Below: **As Marie and Pierre opened the door of their laboratory they saw the faint blue glow of radium.**

One evening in 1902, after four years of exhausting work, Marie and Pierre sat at home in their small, barely-furnished flat. Suddenly Marie decided that she just had to go back to their laboratory to check on the experiments they had done that afternoon. When they got there and opened the door of the old wooden shed they saw a faint blue glow in the darkness – radium!

Although radium can save lives it can also harm. Radiation ulcers like this are quite common if patients are given radiation treatment over a long period of time.

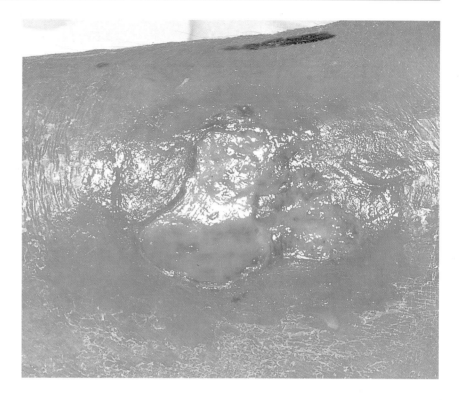

Radium was to prove to be one of the world's great discoveries, especially for its medical uses. It was measured to be two million times more radioactive than uranium. Even a minute quantity, therefore, could give off immense amounts of radioactive energy. Radium was extremely powerful and, unless used with care, very dangerous. Unfortunately, though, this was not realized at the time. While working on radioactive materials both Pierre and Marie suffered many pains and illnesses – aching arms and legs, colds, sores and blisters that never seemed to go away, and a constant feeling of being tired. They both worked very long hours and perhaps put these problems down to overwork and lack of exercise. Occasionally they would take a cycling holiday and feel better.

Only gradually did they come to connect their improvement in their health with their absence from the deadly radium.

Scientists and doctors around the world read about the Curies' great discovery and worked to develop its use. They found that radiation could be used to destroy unhealthy growths in the human body, thus helping to stop cancer.

Radium can help to cure but it can also kill. The problem is how to handle it safely and control its power. And it took time for the Curies to realize this.

The problem that they did recognize was fame. They were quiet people who enjoyed their work and each other's company and asked for nothing more. But their discovery had made them world famous. Many people wanted to learn how to

An illustration showing Marie and Pierre with their great discovery, for which Marie was awarded the degree of Doctor of Science in 1903.

separate radium from pitchblende. The Curies could have taken out a **patent** on their discovery, but they refused to limit the use of knowledge which could possibly save people's lives. In Marie's own words that would have been, "contrary to the scientific spirit."

The discovery of radium did, however, bring the Curies something they did value. In 1903 Marie was awarded the degree of Doctor of Science. At the ceremony where the degree was awarded she showed how much she appreciated the honour by wearing a new dress.

Nobel Prizes

Alfred Nobel (1833–1896) was a Swedish industrialist and the inventor of dynamite. In his will he left the bulk of his vast personal fortune to establish a series of prizes to be awarded each year to the men and women whose work had been of the greatest benefit to the world. Prizes were established for physics, chemistry, medicine, literature and peace. The candidates were to be selected by various Swedish academies and, in the case of peace, by a committee of the Norwegian Parliament. The prizes consisted of a gold medal and a large sum of money. In return the winners were expected to give a public lecture to explain the importance of their work. The Nobel Prizes have lived up to the expectations of their founder and are still regarded as among the highest honours anyone can achieve.

The Swedish industrialist and prize-giver, Alfred Nobel (1833–1896).

An example of the gold medals
awarded to Nobel prize winners
each year.

Honours and awards were now showered upon the Curies. In 1903 Pierre was invited to London to give a lecture about radium. In November of that year the Royal Society, Britain's leading association of scientists, presented Pierre and Marie with one of its highest awards – the Davy Medal. A month later they heard from the Academy of Sciences in Sweden that the Nobel Prize for Physics was to be awarded jointly to the Curies and Henri Becquerel. Marie and Pierre felt too ill to make the journey to Sweden to collect their prize in person and so their friend Becquerel collected their gold medals for them.

The Nobel Prize included a large sum of money – 70,000 gold francs – and the Curies accepted that it would not be "contrary to the scientific spirit" for them to take it. They could use the money to finance further experiments, to release Pierre from teaching so that he could concentrate on research and to repay the kindness and support they had received from their friends and family over the years. They also made gifts to poor Polish students and made a few improvements to their little flat.

But fame had a price which Marie found hard to pay:–

" … Always a hubbub. People are keeping us from work as much as they can. Now I have decided to be brave and I receive no visitors – but they disturb me just the same. Our life has been altogether spoilt by honours and fame … Our peaceful and laborious existence is completely disorganized."

One newcomer that the Curies didn't mind was Eve, their second daughter, born in December 1904. Her arrival did not, however, prevent Marie from re-establishing the old routine of teaching and research and a quiet family life at home. The Curies rarely accepted invitations to formal banquets or receptions, except when they were in honour of fellow scientists from abroad. Then Pierre would put on formal evening dress and Marie would wear her one evening gown.

Above: **Pierre Curie in 1906 shortly before his tragic death.**

Above: **Marie with her daughters, Eve** (left) **and Irène** (right) **in 1908.**

In 1905 Pierre was elected a member of the French Academy of Sciences and became a Professor of Physics at the Sorbonne. Early in the following year tragedy struck. Crossing the road in a shower of rain, Pierre stepped out from behind a cab straight into the path of a heavy horse-drawn wagon. The driver pulled at the reins in vain. The weight of his load was too great for him to stop and the left back wheel of the wagon crushed Pierre as he lay stunned in the road. He died instantly.

Marie was shattered by the news of her husband's death but soon recovered her determination to carry on with her work. When the French government proposed to recognize the value of Pierre's work to the nation by granting her a pension for herself and her children, she refused it saying, "I am young enough to earn my living and that of my children."

Happily the Sorbonne agreed with

In 1906 Marie replaced Pierre at the Sorbonne and became the first ever female professor in France.

Marie's view of her own abilities. The Faculty of Science voted **unanimously** that she should succeed Pierre as Professor. It was a unique tribute, for she thus became not only the first woman professor at the Sorbonne but the first at any French university.

However, Marie was initially troubled by doubts, which she confided to her diary:–

"I am offered the post of successor to you, my Pierre: your course and the direction of your laboratory. I have accepted. I don't know whether this is good or bad. You often told me you would have liked me to give a course at the Sorbonne. And I would like at least to make an effort to continue your work. Sometimes it seems to me that this is how it will be most easy for me to live and at other times it seems to me that I am mad to attempt it."

Marie at last showed her final feelings on the matter by the way in which she gave her first public lecture, to a packed audience. She continued the course at the precise point at which Pierre had left off.

In 1910 Marie published a long account of her discoveries about radioactivity. This led to her being awarded a second Nobel Prize. Not for another 50 years would anyone else achieve such a remarkable honour. This time Marie went to Stockholm in Sweden to collect the prize in person. 1911 should have been a year of triumph, but it turned out to be a year of anguish. Some scientists said Marie should not have been awarded a second prize because

Marie Curie's diploma of her second Nobel prize, awarded to her in 1911.

**The Radium Institute, Paris, built
in the re-named "Rue Pierre Curie".**

other people were also making important discoveries. Others said it was given out of pity for her lost husband, rather than genuine admiration for her own work. In the same year Marie failed by two votes, to be elected to the Academy of Sciences. Worse still, some newspapers said that her close friendship with the scientist Paul Langevin was wrong because he was a married man with four children. Marie received many spiteful letters and became very distressed. A spell in a nursing home and a trip to England helped her to recover.

Marie's real cure for her problems was work. And the Sorbonne at last decided to give her what she needed to do it properly – a special institute for the study of radium, newly-built in a road renamed in honour of her husband, "Rue Pierre Curie". Marie was thrilled with this new project and gave it, as her own personal gift, the precious radium she and Pierre had prepared with their own hands. And precious it was in every sense. It was vital for further scientific research. It was essential for its uses in medicine. And it was worth more than a million gold francs.

The Radium Institute was finished on 13 July 1914. Less than a week later World War I broke out.

Irène Curie

Irène Curie grew up very much in her mother's shadow, yet adored her and continued her work. Marie herself gave her daughter a personal introduction to the mysteries of modern science and the fascination of research. When World War I broke out she had no hesitation in making Irène her personal assistant in organizing X-ray services in the battle zone and leaving her in charge of a unit, even though she was only 17.

After the war Irène's career continued to follow the pattern of her mother's as she proved to be an original researcher in her own right and in 1926 married a distinguished French scientist, Frédéric Joliot (1900–1958). Like Marie and Pierre they became close working partners. For their achievement in discovering how to produce radioactivity artificially they were awarded the Nobel Prize for Chemistry in 1935.

Marie (seated) **with her daughter Irène, working together. Marie taught and encouraged Irène to continue her work with radioactivity.**

Scientist to the World

Marie driving one of her mobile X-ray units, during World War I.

When France found itself at war in 1914 Marie gave up all thought of scientific work in her new institute and threw herself behind the cause of her adopted country. But she still thought about the future and swiftly made a special trip on a troop train to Bordeaux in western France, far away from the fighting, where she put the precious gram of radium safely away in a bank vault.

Marie used the money from her second Nobel Prize to buy war **bonds** which the French government was selling to pay for its military spending. She also took her own small personal savings in gold to the bank to be melted down and used for the war effort. She even offered them her gold medals but the bank refused to accept them.

Marie quickly saw that there was one service she could do for France that no one else could – organize a mass X-ray service for the treatment of wounded soldiers.

Marie's approach to her work was a very direct one. She went straight to rich people and big businesses and asked for what she needed – money, vehicles and medical equipment. She was famous. She was selfless. She was Marie Curie. So they gave.

During the course of the war Marie and her helpers equipped 20 cars as mobile X-ray units and set up more than 200 hospital rooms with X-ray equipment. Medical teams using these facilities X-rayed over a million men, saving tens of thousands of lives and preventing an untold number of amputations by enabling surgeons to find out just where they needed to operate to remove bullets and mend shattered bones. Marie herself visited nearly 400 French and Belgian hospitals in the course of the four years of fighting. At the Radium Institute she also established a course to instruct technicians in the new science she had helped to invent – radiology. Between 1916 and 1918, 150 people were trained in this way, including 20 soldiers from the American Expeditionary Force. Even after the war ended Marie went on training radiologists for another two years. She also wrote a book called *Radiology and War*, which showed how scientific research could be put to practical use to save human life and suffering.

Even in her own book Marie scarcely mentioned her own personal contribution and efforts.

Marie, Irène and radiology students of the American Expeditionary Force.

When Marie finally agreed to travel to the United States, she met many important people, including President Harding.

She disliked publicity and kept away from journalists. But one American reporter, Mrs Marie Meloney, kept on asking for an interview until at last Marie agreed. She was charmed by Mrs Meloney and they became good friends. Mrs Meloney understood how Marie had put aside her scientific work during the war and knew that in the whole of France there was only the one gram of radium that Marie had presented to the newly-established institute.

Mrs Meloney went back to the United States and appealed to the women of her country to raise $100,000 to buy another gram of pure radium for Marie's research and medical use. Such was the admiration that people everywhere felt for "Madame Curie" that the target was soon reached.

In 1921 Marie received an invitation to visit the United States to receive the gram of radium. At first she hesitated, saying that she couldn't leave her young daughters. So Mrs Meloney and her supporters invited them, too. Marie at last overcame her fears and, at the age of 54, for the first time in her life, agreed to be treated like a celebrity.

When her ship docked at New York Marie found that an enormous crowd had been waiting for five hours to welcome her. In Washington she met President Harding who gave her a golden key with which to open the casket containing the radium. But soon the applause and celebrations proved too much for her. She shook so many hands that she had to have her arm

Marie with Dean Pengram of Columbia University.

put in a sling. Marie cut short her visit on doctors' advice and slipped back to France.

According to her daughter, Eve, Marie's trip to the United States changed the direction of her later life. Her own wish might have been to carry on quietly with her own laboratory research. But when she saw the effect that a personal visit or public lecture could have on official support and understanding of a scientific project she decided to take on a new role – **ambassador** for science, travelling to different countries, visiting universities and capital cities, receiving honours and speaking out on behalf of new scientific research.

In Poland, the government also decided to build a radium institute in Warsaw in her honour – the Marie Sklodowska-Curie Institute. In 1925 the President of Poland laid the first cornerstone of the new building. Marie laid the second. The women of the United States saluted her a second time and collected enough money for another gram of radium to be presented to the Polish

The Radium Institute, Warsaw, Poland, erected in Marie Curie's honour in 1925.

MADAME CURIE
NÉE SOPHIE CLAIRE
DEPOULLY
1832 – 1897

PIERRE CURIE
1859 – 1906

EUGÈNE CURIE
1827 – 1910

Ⅱ CURIE-SKŁODOWSKA
1867 – 1934

The Curies' family tomb where Marie was buried on 6 July 1934 next to her husband who died in 1906, leaving her a widow for 28 years.

Institute for its own research and treatment programme. In 1929 Marie again sailed for the United States and stayed at the White House as President Hoover's guest for another presentation ceremony.

Amid her public duties Marie continued with her own research but her health was clearly beginning to fail. Years of experimenting with radium and exposure to X-rays during the war damaged her blood and caused annoying and painful burns on her hands. Her sight, too, began to fade rapidly until she was almost blind.

In May 1934, Marie took to her bed with an attack of influenza. She was too weak to fight off the infection and died in a sanatorium in the French Alps. She was buried quietly, without any official ceremony, on 6 July 1934, and laid to rest beside her beloved Pierre.

Find Out More ...

Important Dates

1867 Born, Manya Sklodowska
1878 Death of her mother
1882 Wins gold medal
1886 Joins Zorawski family as a governess
1891 Arrives in Paris
1895 Marries Pierre Curie
1897 Birth of Irène
1902 Achieves isolation of radium
1903 Becomes Doctor of Science and wins Nobel Prize
1904 Birth of Eve
1906 Death of Pierre; Marie becomes a professor at the Sorbonne
1910 Publishes *Treatise on Radioactivity*
1911 Wins second Nobel Prize
1914 Radium Institute completed; Sets up wartime X-ray service
1916 Begins training courses for radiologists
1921 Visit to the United States
1925 Dedication of Warsaw Radium Institute
1929 Second trip to the United States
1934 Dies

Useful Information

Curie Institute
26 rue d'Ulm
75005 Paris
France
www.musee.curie.fr

Marie Curie Cancer Care
89 Albert Embankment
London
SE1 7TP
www.mariecurie.org.uk

Marie Curie Fellowship Association
International Office
Université Libre de Bruxelles
28 Avenue Roosevelt
13-1050 Bruxelles
Belgium
www.mariecurie.org

Science Museum, The
Exhibition Road
South Kensington
London
SW7 2DD
www.sciencemuseum.org.uk/ collections/exhiblets/curie

The Nobel Foundation
Box 5232, SE-102 45
Stockholm
Sweden
www.nobel.se/physics/laureates/ 1903/marie-curie-bio.htm

Glossary

Ambassador   An official, sent by a government to a foreign country, to make its views known and look after its interests.

Bonds   Certificates sold by governments to raise money; after a period of time, they can be sold back to the government at a higher price.

Consecrated   Devoted to a single act or task, leaving no time for anything else.

Governess   A private female teacher appointed to educate the children of a family in their own home.

Mineral   A lifeless substance such as a rock or metal.

Patent   A legal document giving an inventor the right to prevent other people using a new invention without payment.

Perseverance   Following a task or goal right through to the end.

Properties   Qualities that make one substance different from another. E.g., hardness.

Purifying   Making a substance free of other substances by removing them.

Thorium   A radioactive element.

Tuberculosis   A disease of the lungs, often caused by bad living conditions, which can be fatal.

Unanimously   A decision made without anyone disagreeing.

Uranium   A radioactive element much used in the production of atomic power.

Index

American Expeditionary Force 25

Becquerel, Antoine Henri 11,12,18
    Nobel Prize for Physics 18
Belgium 25
Britain 18
    England 22
    London 18
    Royal Society 18

Curie, Eve 19,28
Curie, Irène 11,23
Curie, Marie
    awards 4,16,18,21
    birth 4
    Manya Sklodowska 4,5,6,7
    father 4,5
    mother 4,5
    education 4,5,6
    governess 6-7
    teaching 7,13,19,20,21
    studying in Paris 8
    scholarship 8
    marriage 8,10
    cycling holidays 10,15
    scientific research 10,11,12,13,14,19,22,25,28,29
    studying uranium 11,12
    studying pitchblende 12,13
    laboratory 14
    discovering radium 14,15,16
    illnesses 15,28,29
    fame 15,18,24
    Doctor of Science 16
    Davy Medal 18
    Nobel Prize for Physics 18
    Professor of Physics 20
    lecturing 21,28
    writing 21,25
    Nobel Prize for Chemistry 21,24
    X-ray service 23,24,25
    teaching radiology 25
    Radiology and War 25
    travel 27,28,29
    ambassador for science 28
    death 29
Curie, Pierre 9,12,13,14,15,19,20,21,23,29

Dluski, Casimir 7

France 4,5,10,23,24,25,26,28

Alps 29
Bordeaux 23
Paris
French Academy of Sciences 19,22

Harding, President 27
Hoover, President 29

Joliot, Frédéric 23

Langevin, Paul 22

Meloney, Mrs Marie 26,27

Nobel Prizes 4,17,18,21,23,24
    Nobel, Alfred 17

pitchblende 12,16
Poland 4,5,13,18
    Warsaw 28
polonium 13

radioactivity 12,15,21
radiology 25
radium 12,13,14,15,16,18,24,26,27,29
Radium Institute, Paris 22,25,26
Radium Institute, Warsaw 28-9
Roentgen, Wilhelm 10,11
    X-rays 10,11,23,29
Russia 4

Sèvres 13
Ecole Normale Supérieure 13
Sklodowska, Bronya 5,6,7,8
Sklodowska, Sofia 5
Sorbonne University 6,7,8,19,20,21,22
    School of Physics and Chemistry 9,12
Sweden 18,21
    Academy of Sciences 18
    Stockholm 21

thorium 12

United States 26,27,28,29
    New York 27
    Washington 27
uranium 11,15

World War I 22,23,24,25,26,29

Picture Acknowledgements

The publishers would like to thank the following for providing the photographs and illustrations in this book: Mary Evans Picture Library Cover, frontispiece, 16,17,18,20; Science Photo Library 10 (top), 12,15. The illustrations were provided by Simon Roulestone.